Call of the Moon

Srividya Suryanarayanan

BookLeaf Publishing

India | USA | UK

Presentation by *BookLeaf Publishing*

Web: www.bookleafpub.com

E-mail: info@bookleafpub.com

ISBN: 9789363300460

First edition 2024

For Amma and Appa

ACKNOWLEDGEMENT

My Late Parents' blessings remain with me and reflect in my poems.

My siblings and cousins have been a great support in this journey.

My sincere thanks to my Professor/Mentor Judith Serin, an author and a poet living in San Francisco, California. Her critiques of my poems were clear and meticulous. It helped me to fashion the poems' basic version.

Cheerful Smitha Bala Aiyar, who is a family friend, had taken the author's photo used in the Back Cover.

This collection started out as part of BookLeaf Publishing's initiative of their 21-day Poetry Challenge.

I'm thankful to the team of BookLeaf Publishing. Shivani Jhawar (Assigned Consultant), Shikha (the Poems' Editor), and Hemapriya P (Book's Graphic Designer).

This book became a reality because of all the involved people's contributions. I am thankful for it, while being humbled by the loving support that I received from all.

PREFACE

I would like to begin with an invocation to my muse. The prime deity in the Hindu way of life is Lord Ganesha. His presence at the start of any work promises a well-intended completion. Here is a take on the inspiring Muse of mine.

Rotund Deity of Wisdom

Moments, when I see You,
Like the early morning dew,
Like a gentle thought membrane,

You comfort me with your grace,
Like a happy babe in the cradle,
Like a smile on the ageing visages,

Your wisdom spreads delight
Inside my sorrow-filled heart—while
Surrounded by endearing things.

You are the resident being,
Swept by your caring gaze,
My benediction, I put forth,

Gather me in your maternal hands,
Gently then ease the pain I feel—While
Lost in endless vain objects.

Mislaid in an illusionary world.
I might be drowned in aplenty—as
You carry me securely in my strife.

In the thirsty human memory,
Your presence is a well of relief,
Sorting out life's complex plans.

You are my blameless routes—that
I took against my life's challenges—As
The essence of You lives in my being.

The Search is on, for that living deity,
Perchance to work out my Karma,
To equal my good and bad deeds.

Deep transitory spirit's wisdom fires,
Rekindles the spiritual awareness—as I know
You, me, and my work are, but same.

Why Villanelles?!

After reading Dylan Thomas' villanelle, a need arose to explore the poetic form. Creating them is still an immense surreal joy.

The satisfaction of writing a villanelle lies in overcoming the challenges of rhyming skills. The structured form creates a forced limit to end rhymes and has a set rhyming sequence throughout the poem.

The poem's charm emulates when the refrains' beat hits spot on. It creates a uniqueness in every single stanza.

Here, in these poems are my version of the Moon and its nocturnal hunts set to an internal rhyming scheme.

The Villanelle originated as songs for dancing in Italy. Later, during the Renaissance literary movement the French Poet Théodore de Banville (1823 - 1891) gave it the present-day structured form.

The repetition of the first and third lines of the first, three lined stanza or tercet sets to motion the movements within the poem.

The rhyme patterns for the six stanzas poem
with 5 Tercets and 1 Quatrain are as follows:
1st Tercet (A1 b A2),
2nd Tercet (a b A1),
3rd Tercet (a b A2),
4th Tercet (a b A1),
5th Tercet (a b A2), and
6th Quatrain (a b A1 A2).

The rhyming lines of A1 and A2 in the First
Tercet act as a refrain that underlines the
experience of each stanza. While (a, b) words
rhyming is kept at a slightly different pace.

I am hoping that the reader of the collection will
find some of my poems entertaining. I wish, as
you are reading them, you find the connections
of the Moon and other cultural elements in the
poem.

The Elephantine God

Benevolent graces that often stretch,
Across the horizon where all is one,
Lights the way, for the self to fetch.

Within a warm care of sunshine,
Those tiny resolves we get done,
Benevolent graces that often stretch,

Watching, the shores of life's line,
An incredible moment got on loan,
Lights the way, for the self to fetch.

Vortex of energy openings are nine,
In the Soul's citadels are they born,
Benevolent graces that often stretch,

Everything now is in Mist of Time,
On shores of wisdom long worn,
Lights the way, for the self to fetch.

Primaeval deity common, yet Divine!
His splendid grace pairs to none,
Benevolent graces that often stretch,
Lights the way, for the self to fetch.

Her Nightly Errand

Passionate Moon overlooks its find,
And bestows her calming glance,
Hearts are made of love, full and kind.

Slumber settles in our head,
Afloat on dream-found trance,
Passionate Moon overlooks its find,

Drunk with dreamy subplots I read,
Hastens then, the strange set dance,
Hearts are made of love, full and kind.

A lone piper drifted on to lead
Towards the right ways perchance,
Passionate Moon overlooks its find,

Wild wind picks up debris ahead,
Screaming as it pliantly advance,
Hearts are made of love, full and kind.

Last night spent rolling prayer beads,
Hunger kept at bay by a slim chance,
Passionate Moon overlooks its find,
Hearts are made of love, full and kind.

Witness of Love

Full or New Moon equally saw,
All that humans knew about love,
Marking each piece a master's law.

The childhood's sweet blossoms,
Nightly dream that fits like a glove,
Full or New Moon equally saw,

Confused or lost in flotsam,
Gaining, but a false Ludu love,
Marking each piece a master's law.

Delving into the dream's bottom,
Carrying emotions from above,
Full or New Moon equally saw,

Following moments are solemn,
Leaving a pattern never to dissolve,
Marking each piece a master's law.

Dive deep into the nightly fathom,
Find an endearing but safe cove,
Full or New Moon equally saw,
Marking each piece a master's law.

Queen of Matchmaking

As lifelong commitments fail,
Vanishing as bubbles in space,
Showcase false love is but frail.

In the thunderstorm or the hail,
Love leaves but a faint trace,
As lifelong commitments fail,

Love's flower withered and pale,
Wrapped in pink and red lace,
Showcase false love is but frail.

Her impossible matching tale,
A true celestial love, just in case,
As lifelong commitments fail,

She sparks the heart to trail
Along the lover's true grace,
Showcase false love is but frail.

So, find in your heart scale,
Among true moment's place,
As lifelong commitments fail,
Showcase false love is but frail.

Undeviating Life and Death

Birth and Death are the celestial take,
Night sky revolves with the fated stars,
After all, it is only a sad human mistake.

Repeated human errors often do make,
Jostled out as these minor scars,
Birth and Death are the celestial take,

Soft whispers are from cold memory lake,
Hear the Universe speak of cruel Czars,
After all, it is only a sad human mistake.

Each Moon cycle, she refused to break,
Her ice-cold emotions repeat to jar,
Birth and Death are the celestial take,

While peace, we completely forsake,
Soul's injuries leave marks of war,
After all, it is only a sad human mistake.

As troubles of humanity lay awake,
Chained and drowning sorrow in a bar,
Birth and Death are the celestial take,
After all, it is only a sad human mistake.

The Heart's Phases

As Moon's phases by change humbled,
Heart carries the memories that fall,
As midnight's corners roughly tumbled.

Love's fists worn with bruised knuckles,
Human affection lost in portion small,
As Moon's phases by change humbled,

Heartfelt love hugs are but cuddles,
Forgive or forget heated verbal brawl,
As midnight's corners roughly tumbled.

Life's records found in heart's muscles,
While hurting, we dare to fake a drawl,
As Moon's phases by change humbled,

When the lonesome seeking heart juggles,
Emotions hidden inside muscled wall,
As midnight's corners roughly tumbled.

All night, the lone souls guard the shovel,
Illusion of love, then becomes a scrawl,
As Moon's phases by change humbled,
As midnight's corners roughly tumbled.

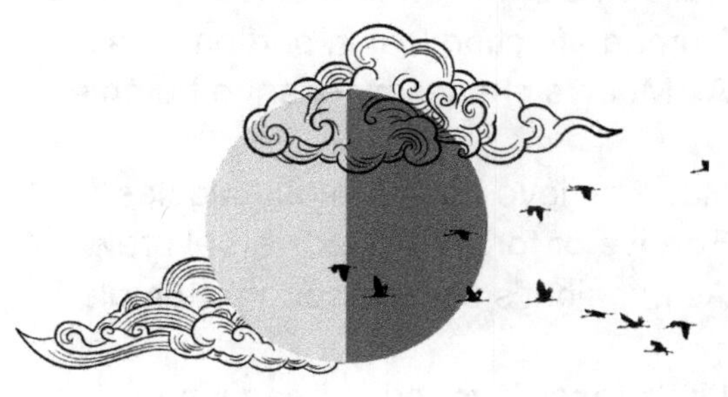

Night-Raider of Dreamscape

Night-Raider seeks to shake,
Confidence is but a scar,
Then what does that make?

Purple hearts missed a take,
Care, then, is that single mar,
Night-Raider seeks to shake,

Worry, a constant headache
Our woes engage in a spar,
Then what does that make?

A drunk rat of first heartbreak,
Of jointly spent times so far,
Night-Raider seeks to shake,

Redress never for heartache,
But left to stretch on the tar,
Then what does that make?

It is time for us to awake
Start once again on par,
Night-Raider seeks to shake,
Then what does that make?

Sprites of Moonlight

A blighted Moon shines bright,
Making creative minds go wild,
Cavorting with those nightly sprites.

Night's written word hold tight,
Dreaming away like a child,
A blighted Moon shines bright,

Every syllable felt just and right!
Next day, all words begin to slide,
Cavorting with those nightly sprites.

Casting shadows on the pen's might,
Hiding in papers' folds, dreams piled,
A blighted Moon shines bright,

Her dreamscapes left me in a sight,
Tempered in Bohemian style filed,
Cavorting with those nightly sprites.

Words' extravagant big fight,
In the mind's eyes they tiled,
A blighted Moon shines bright,
Cavorting with those nightly sprites.

Oneiroi's Visit to Night Land

Night rules are but loose law,
As his nightly expanse of love,
Based on whatever you saw!

Raven eats away the soul raw,
In darkness mistaken for a dove,
Night rules are but loose law,

The mad crackling of a cat's paw.
Night's vision then begin to shove
Based on whatever you saw!

Onlookers' dream a huge haw,
Is a pleasant gift from above!
Night rules are but loose law,

Drawing children in joyous awe,
Cooking up on an imaginary stove,
Based on whatever you saw!

For the Autumn, the last straw,
Winter left to trace and resolve,
Night rules are but loose law,
Based on whatever you saw!

Pan's Dream Snarl

Nocturnal ventures, often defined.
Like a mediaeval sharp lance,
Leaving us in pain undefined.

Our differences when combined,
Into an understanding perchance,
Nocturnal ventures, often defined.

Of the Nightly pact we signed,
Giving our blood as advance,
Leaving us in pain undefined.

Pogey peace are often kept lined,
A ration of dream snarl we glance,
Nocturnal ventures, often defined.

Black dream boxes are blind,
Seeking a way out by chance,
Leaving us in pain undefined.

Pan's snarl dreams help us find,
That mixed wilderness dance,
Nocturnal ventures, often defined.
Leaving us in pain undefined.

Buddha Poornima

Humans do inadvertently stumble,
On emotional issues on the way,
Like Buddha, carry a bowl humble.

When life seems a lasting grumble,
Path ahead will then, in darkness stay,
Humans do inadvertently stumble,

Facing challenges we may crumble,
Our worried souls begin to fray,
Like Buddha, carry a bowl humble.

Empty all that negative mumble,
As unpinned thoughts stray,
Humans do inadvertently stumble,

Peace slips away and we fumble,
In the River Hades, all seem gay,
Like Buddha, carry a bowl humble.

Nightly dream are but a juggle,
While the emotions would sway,
Humans do inadvertently stumble,
Like Buddha, carry a bowl humble.

Midsummer Night's Dream

Fancy-free dreams are in sight,
The mind flips over and goes wild,
Grooving to an unusual disco night.

As eventide wound down tight,
In morn, it wakes as a reborn child,
Fancy-free dreams are in sight,

Pan's dreams set the stage alight,
They seemed to be just and mild,
Grooving to an unusual disco night.

Failing eyes see a vision bright,
Left with a smirk line that smiled,
Fancy-free dreams are in sight,

Wandering off, left alone in fright,
Dancing bare and in craze riled,
Grooving to an unusual disco night.

Midsummer calls all to light,
My life craves to be freestyle,
Fancy-free dreams are in sight,
Grooving to an unusual disco night.

Primaeval Moon

Moon's scars become night's game,
Her cycles never were an oversight,
Reflecting on Earth a cooler flame.

A lone flute, call it by any other name,
Sound shimmers out of the backlight,
Moon's scars become night's game,

Hiding within the subtle human shame,
Let disagreement slide off fistfight,
Reflecting on Earth a cooler flame.

Dreams manifest as short fake fame,
Sad images beam like flashlight,
Moon's scars become night's game,

Seems whacky dreams are but lame,
Harsh reality turns into a fierce bullfight,
Reflecting on Earth a cooler flame.

With daybreak, all things new came,
At nightfall vanishes with daylight,
Moon's scars become night's game,
Reflecting on Earth a cooler flame.

Blue Moon

Blue Moon happens to be a spell short,
While tracing countless rebirth boons,
Strapped within, yet be a physical fort.

Our experiences become naught,
Endless race with lemon and spoon,
Blue Moon happens to be a spell short,

Night magic captured in snug thought,
In darkness found an immoral goon,
Strapped within, yet be a physical fort.

Wild Moon in ethical desire sort,
The pick of the maids who swoon,
Blue Moon happens to be a spell short,

Four castle rides childhood bought,
For a Moon so Blue do they croon,
Strapped within, yet be a physical fort.

In the eyes of a virgin maid caught,
Sparkling moments from ageing noon,
Blue Moon happens to be a spell short,
Strapped within, yet be a physical fort.

Blood Moon

Strife always in stealth arrived,
Drive-off peace attempt by the guild,
Then, achieving peace is stalled.

While discord around us purred,
Dancing like a restrained child,
Strife always in stealth arrived,

On Blood Moon, talks turn absurd,
For petition of well-being piled,
Then, achieving peace is stalled.

Lawful talk's thought is blurred,
Calmer words become a fair child,
Strife always in stealth arrived,

Anger, high in confusion, stirred,
Crashing Death tolls are filed,
Then, achieving peace is stalled.

Peace, a lip service of the herd,
While evil smirked and smiled,
Strife always in stealth arrived,
Then, achieving peace is stalled.

Mythical Moons

While riding on Her high command,
Fine spun world's debates set ablaze
Loyalty for life, Her sole demand.

Bad cards flip now in Her able-hand,
She keeps a steady and sharp gaze,
While riding on Her high command,

Immortal Deities who understand,
Take pleasure from all that emblaze,
Loyalty for life, Her sole demand.

As Her nightly minions on land
Divide and conquer each phase,
While riding on Her high command,

Nightly errands authorise Rand,
Creating illusions that are haze,
Loyalty for life, Her sole demand.

Dreams drain the hour sand,
Her minions drew us into a maze,
While riding on Her high command,
Loyalty for life, Her sole demand.

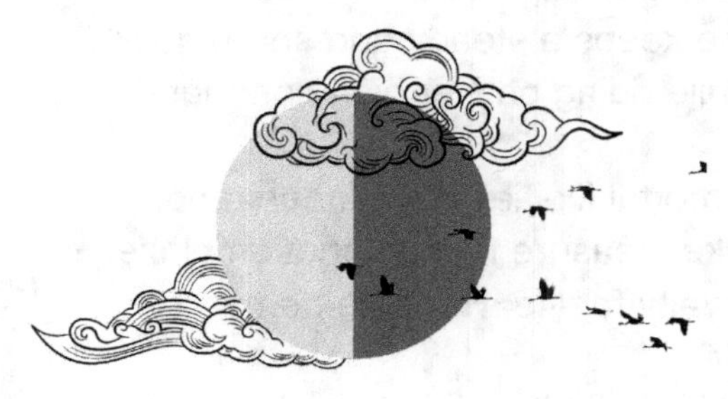

Pan and Horus Party

Diurnal images of concrete jungle,
As Night Gods turn and swing,
In a trance state does life juggle.

Time away, wakes Her prime,
Often gathering at the dream's spring,
Diurnal images of concrete jungle,

Piper's sharp notes are a crime,
Flying past the drunk Druid wing,
In a trance state does life juggle.

Horus is not that far, spicing time,
Horror and freakish breakups bring,
Diurnal images of concrete jungle.

Drawing from within human slime,
The marking of desolate dowsing,
In a trance state does life juggle.

Struggling soul silently mime,
While they are done struggling,
Diurnal images of concrete jungle,
In a trance state does life juggle.

Cornered Love Moon

Two beings fit each other like gloves,
Their emotions are nicely entwined,
They are as close as peaceful doves.

Could this be then, those true loves,
That fluttering hearts do not mind,
Two beings fit each other like gloves,

Moon shines on secret groves,
A table of plenty was set and dined,
They are as close as peaceful doves.

Confessions need a human shove
Chambers of sound, where they pined,
Two beings fit each other like gloves,

Cornered hearts beat in droves,
Prayers hidden and safely enshrined
They are as close as peaceful doves.

Her cool petals drift down on coves,
Drunk in their night's dream, they wined,
Two beings fit each other like gloves,
They are as close as peaceful doves.

Eclipsed Baku-San Moon

Baku-san has eaten dreams to keep,
Until those dark fears are too beat,
Let Him not take my hopes deep.

Into those nightmares, we seep,
Blood curdles in colours of beet,
Baku-san has eaten dreams to keep,

Life's dark shade climbs and creeps,
The beast gently appeals in a bleat,
Let Him not take my hopes deep.

Our pains are but, a cowering sheep,
And our nocturnal trips will meet,
Baku-san has eaten dreams to keep,

Shadows of risqué dreams beep,
In folds swept and tidied neat,
Let Him not take my hopes deep.

For those sad thoughts do I weep,
As I wallowed for my hope sweet,
Baku-san has eaten dreams to keep,
Let Him not take my hopes deep.

Soulmate Moon

While search has been a wild goal,
It drives the mind to an unbridled spot,
Hearts then crave for a kindred soul.

Dig the soul and make a big hole,
Hope is the chance that wait and clot,
While search has been a wild goal,

But all those collections, I stole,
Rethink of what new things I got,
Hearts then crave for a kindred soul.

Mind muddled and sunk in a hole,
Rattling out an endearing old plot,
While search has been a wild goal,

Tracing with confidence, I'm on a roll,
Creating sequences of lost-love slot,
Hearts then crave for a kindred soul.

My mind shoos off hope from my soul,
Every time, when I say, "give it a shot!"
While search has been a wild goal,
Hearts then crave for a kindred soul.

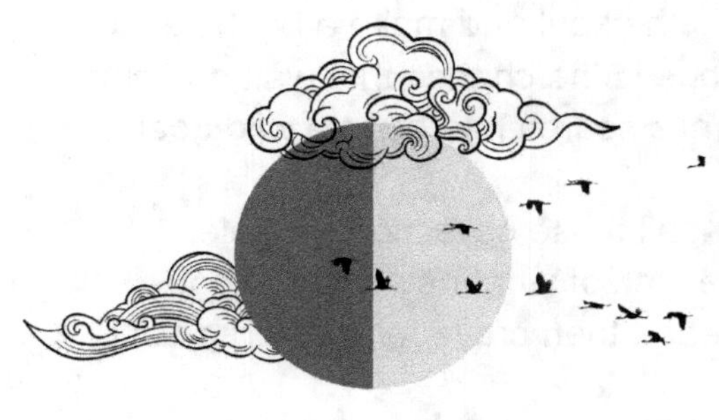

Moon's Invisible Heart

42

Silent remains the heart never,
Hidden in the muscled cave,
Seeks to create a life that's better.

Beating Moon sings along forever
Amid the pain, the partner gave,
Silent remains the heart never,

Encased memories we remember,
Like the precious stones we save.
Seeks to create a life that's better.

Right in the moments together,
Creating such a huge tidal wave,
Silent remains the heart never,

Nightly visits are so like Her!
Finding or losing, yet be brave,
Seeks to create a life that's better.

Light breeze calls me over
In my past lives' close shave,
Silent remains the heart never,
Seeks to create a life that's better.

Red Fox, Fire, and Blue Moon

Left to devise a plan, I would then stare,
Musing on my pasts and those old ways
Howling happily, while my red coat flares.

A few moments of steep trance share,
A rapture-driven in the mind-body stay.
Left to devise a plan, I would then stare,

In that dark side on the mountain rare,
A camper lights a fire to end a day.
Howling happily, while my red coat flares.

The silver lining that I sometimes wear,
When around the Blue Moon, I'm an array!
Left to devise a plan, I would then stare,

All those fears within me begin to dare,
While in deep earnestness do I pray,
Howling happily, while my red coat flares.

I frizzle, my hair stands out in a flair,
A teasing rabbit on the Moon seen at play,
Left to devise a plan, I would then stare,
Howling happily, while my red coat flares.

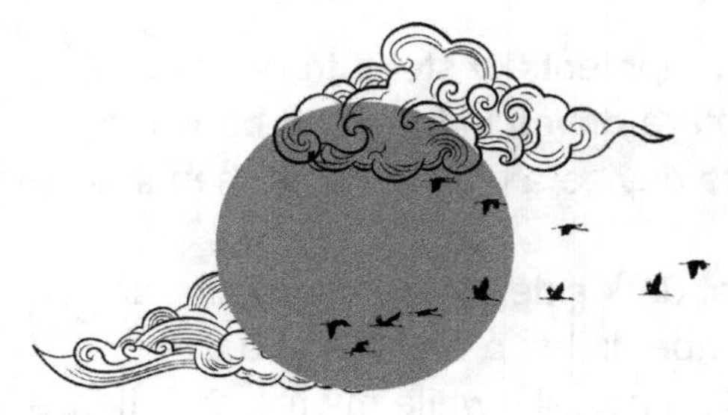

The Moon Who Laughed

Mistakes of mocking and laughing,
But then, content was my festive meal,
Torn tummy and an accidental spilling.

Yet, that mocking ways infuriating,
Scaled His depth of angry weal,
Mistakes of mocking and laughing,

Sure, miscreant wouldn't be stopping,
Roaring rage builds, trembled for real,
Torn tummy and an accidental spilling.

Primaeval and celestial beings moving,
Locked their eyes as anger soon seal,
Mistakes of mocking and laughing,

Rotund deity's anger now sheathing,
Claimed the better part of the deal,
Torn tummy and an accidental spilling.

For too late to realise, error of laughing,
Couldn't seek to stage an appeal,
Mistakes of mocking and laughing,
Torn tummy and an accidental spilling.

Call of the Moon

Mysterious night's elemental sound,
Chosen moments will be transformed,
Echoes through vale and dale surround.

Last night's gathering still found,
Those being who never changed,
Mysterious night's elemental sound,

Graces that spoke from high ground,
Of lesions on fair maiden exchanged,
Echoes through vale and dale surround.

Green pastures where the music abound,
While cowherds and their cattle grazed,
Mysterious night's elemental sound,

Traces of pastoral life's affection bound,
Like a fine handmade quilt well-laced,
Echoes through vale and dale surround.

Long shadows of moon can be found,
Covering grounds that were tossed,
Mysterious night's elemental sound,
Echoes through vale and dale surround.

Mama Quilla of Quechuans

For Mama Quilla was a nurturing mother,
Over Her subjects, She wisely ruled,
As they remained safe and free of bother.

When in a moment heavy and bitter
With a pure heart, our flaws She shed,
For Mama Quill was a nurturing mother,

Lunar cycles stirred the calendar glitter.
To pursue changes that She reasoned,
As they remained safe and free of bother.

Ageing wines in the leather casks cater,
As nightly festive jubilation gathered,
For Mama Quilla was a nurturing mother,

Among the various pranks of player
A benevolent gaze fell on and urged,
As they remained safe and free of bother.

Quechuans then, joined the night lair,
Where their joy and happiness led.
For Mama Quilla was a nurturing mother,
As they remained safe and free of bother.

Secrets of Moonwater

Moon and Women are different, yet same,
Secrets deep and complex, She thrives,
But in weird circles, they appear as a game.

Support life's wilderness and to tame,
Throwing past glories on steep archives,
Moon and Women are different, yet same,

Yet these moon cycles a social shame,
She bottles up all emotion with a shive,
But in weird circles, they appear as a game.

Clearing, creating, as the Moon's claim,
Tarnished and garnished by five senses,
Moon and Women are different, yet same,

Without a title, She, but all overcame,
The Queen Bee of her personal hive,
But in weird circles, they appear as a game.

Life grows, expands, sets her aflame,
Working day and night for her beehive,
Moon and Women are different, yet same,
But in weird circles, they appear as a game.

Harvest Full Moon

Autumnal equinox brings familial joy,
Remembers the pouring sands of past,
To tell us, living is an illusionary ploy.

Lunar month celebrations are an alloy,
Prayers spoken as an ancestral repast,
Autumnal equinox brings familial joy,

Songpyeon turns pretentious and coy,
Until one and all, to even youngest last,
To tell us, living is an illusionary ploy.

Young hands at harvest are in employ,
To gather again to make *Kimchi* fast,
Autumnal equinox brings familial joy,

Silver lining of moonlight deploy,
Shivers of wealth are forever cast,
To tell us, living is an illusionary ploy.

Moonlight then, all sadness destroys,
Masking the night in joyous forecast,
Autumnal equinox brings familial joy,
To tell us, living is an illusionary ploy.

Tumultuous Oceans

Tumultuous ocean seems to clash,
Promenades on rocky shores entice,
Floodgate, the Moon churns only to smash.

Collecting sand from faraway stash,
Water is charged in vigorous disguise,
Tumultuous ocean seems to clash,

Discords on the overnight hightide lash,
Merchant ships' fortune are left to dice,
Floodgate, the Moon churns only to smash.

On stormy nights, coastal faith is rash,
Debris on the shores, rich in price,
Tumultuous oceans seems to clash,

Six Indian seasons change and mash,
Spells of Fishing as a living, is a slice,
Floodgate, the Moon churns only to smash.

Salts made on the shore are black ash,
Sprinkled on dried fish and cooked rice
Tumultuous ocean seems to clash,
Floodgate, the Moon churns only to smash.

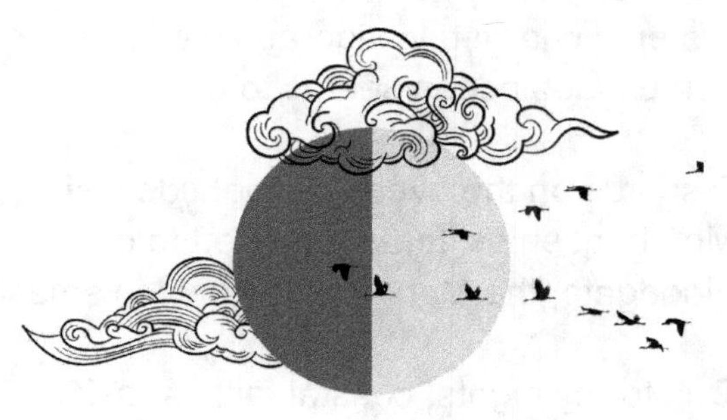

The Moon Followed Me

I travelled through the night terrain,
Wondering and fending for myself
And then, the Moon followed me again.

From every window, a glimpse attains,
Recreating splendour within myself,
I travelled through the night terrain,

In a cool breeze on high sky, she reigns
Capturing the beating hearts left on shelf,
And then, the Moon followed me again.

On the BART, then CalTrain, when in pain,
Moving fast or slow, I reflect on myself,
I travelled through the night terrain,

At the station, when in a pun refrain,
Is the Moon hiding or am Her elf?
And then, the Moon followed me again.

Parts of a complex personality remain,
The changes within me often help,
I travelled through the night terrain,
And then, the Moon followed me again.

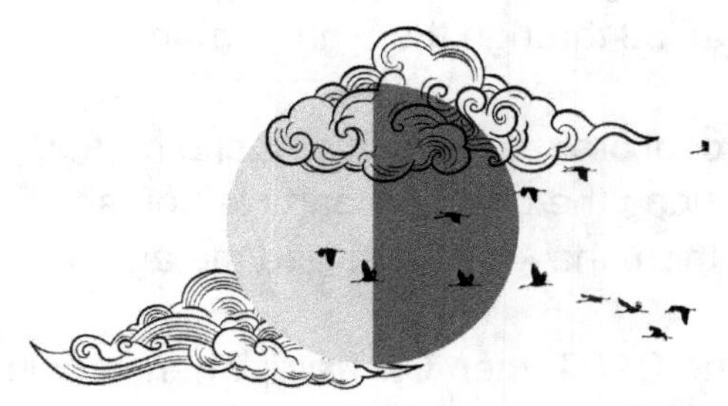

Nocturnal Psyche of Moon

Once the Moon became my dream,
In awestruck wonder was I seen,
Everything was but a positive stream.

Vegetables and Fruits in party scheme,
Amidst them, I sat all alert and keen,
Once the Moon became my dream,

Sun and Moon in a love story gleam,
I am an involuntary audience in a scene.
Everything was but a positive stream.

The good witch shined in moonbeam,
Promised the bride splendid sheen,
Once the Moon became my dream,

Slowly the guests arrived as esteemed,
The Fairy Godmother was truly green,
Everything was but a positive stream.

Evil Sorceress would curse and scream,
Silent Godmother's blessings, all seen,
Once the Moon became my dream,
Everything was but a positive stream.